A Creative Writing Course

Book 1: Get Started

Diny van Kleeff

Author, poet and creative writing teacher

www.dinyfvk.co.uk

BOOKS (AVAILABLE ON AMAZON)

FREEN: The First Truth

Crime and Cremation

A Nurturing Way to Teach your Child to Read

Copyright © January 2020 Diny van Kleeff
Cover photograph by Photo by Amador Loureiro on Unsplash
All rights reserved.
ISBN: 9781656739278

Before you begin this course

- The course is listed by week, but not everyone has the time to dedicate each week, so please don't feel bad if you replace weeks with months or longer – the main thing is that you are doing it, which means your writing WILL be improving.

- Keep everything you write (even if you hate it, or think it is terrible) – all the exercises you do so that you can look back over them and improve them as your writing skills increase.

- Don't be discouraged if you do not get on with a particular exercise, or it isn't something you want to write. By all means write something entirely different - as long as you are writing, that is a good thing. However, I would encourage you to step out of your comfort zone from time to time because you may find a new genre, or technique that you didn't realise you loved until you tried it.

- Enjoy writing and be proud of it, whatever level you are starting at and know that every time you write, you will understand the craft of writing better.

- Read more and look at the books you read from the point of view of a writer and ask, why did the author do it that way?

- This course is based on the real-life creative writing courses I run and my aim is to keep introducing different ideas and techniques for you to try out each week, for you to add to your writing skills repertoire.

What should you write on?

I would encourage you to use a computer, rather than paper and pen because it allows you to edit more easily and if you are looking to publish, or self-publish, your writing will need to be typed. However, if you only like pen and paper, then by all means keep using it.

Personally, I use Microsoft Word because it has everything I need to produce books like this one but, there are specialist writing software packages that have good reputations, if you wish to invest in one.

Course contents

Week 1 — How do I become a writer?
The five finger pitch

Week 2 — What does dialogue do?
Writing good dialogue

Week 3 — Point of View
Character Profiles

Week 4 — Tenses
Writing Pace

Week 5 — Poetic devices

Week 6 — Launch into Poetry

Week 7 — What turns words into poetry?
Poem forms
Poetic clichés

Week 8 — Theme & Genre

Week 9 — Hooks
Cliffhangers

Week 10 — Frame Stories

Week 11 — Colour a scene

Week 12 — Thinking about writing for children

One last thing — Rich Writing Bingo

Notes — Plots & Masterplans
Novel ideas
Stories I must write
Writing competitions

Week 1

Before you get started, it is worthwhile noting that there are certain, pre-set expectations (from both readers and publishers) for the word-count of different genres or types of book. Numbers vary slightly, according to source, but are approximately:

TYPE OF WRITING / BOOKS	WORD COUNT
Standard Novel	80,000 to 100,000
Young Adult Novel	45,000 to 80,000
Science Fiction Novel	100,000 to 125,000
Literary Fiction	55,000 to 100,000
First Chapter books	4,000 to 10,000
Middle Grade Fiction (ages 9-12)	30,000 to 55,000
Novella	17,500 to 39,999
Novelette	7,500 to 17,499
Short Story	under 7,500
Flash Fiction	Usually under 2500
Flash 500	500
Twitter story	280 CHARACTERS
Zines (hand-printed A5 magazines – you can see lots of examples on Etsy.com – great for poetry.)	About 24 x A5 pages
Articles for magazines	100 to 750 – or more
Blog post	Any length but around 2000 is preferred by readers.

Whether you are considering self, or mainstream publishing, it is worth sticking within these guidelines until you are established.

How do I become a writer?

Do you mean, someone who makes a living from writing, or someone who writes for pleasure?

If you want to make a living from being a writer, then there is a huge amount you should learn about *'The Business of Writing'* and there are lots of websites and YouTube tutorials that can help you, but first, you need to get writing – because the way to get good at writing is to write – A LOT.

Why? Because writing is a craft, and like any craft – the more you do it, the better you get. Just take a look at the very first novels of many well-known writers. Quite often you will see a marked difference in their ability, style and confidence.

Writers also:

- Subscribe to writing magazines, such as **Writing Magazine** (*www.writers-online.co.uk*) or **Writers Forum** (*www.writers-forum.com*).
- Attend local Literary Festivals – most towns have them and they are great places to chat to other authors and people in the business of writing and publishing.
- Join Facebook groups for writers and writing groups, which provide excellent support, information and useful resources.
- Attend a writing group. There may be several in your area, so try them out and find a group that is a good fit for YOU, because they each have different 'personalities'.

But, most important of all

Write. A lot.

Week 1

The Five Finger Pitch

A story has five essential elements. If you miss one of these elements, you will probably not have a complete, or satisfying story to tell.

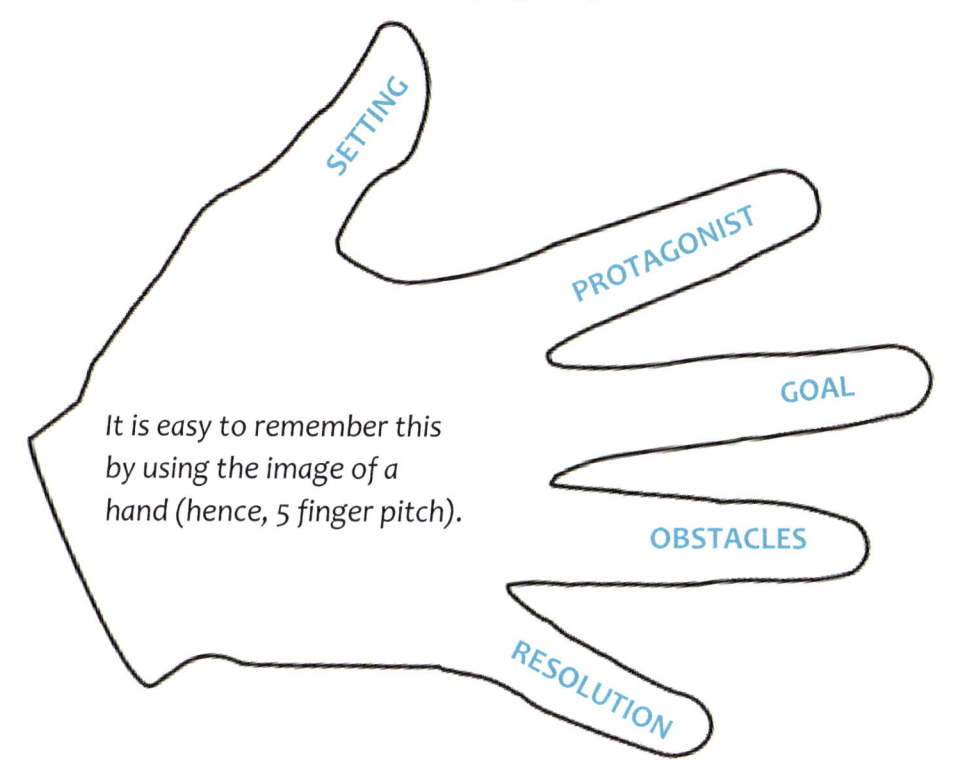

It is easy to remember this by using the image of a hand (hence, 5 finger pitch).

- SETTING
- PROTAGONIST
- GOAL
- OBSTACLES
- RESOLUTION

SETTING (time period and/or location) - is the story set in a specific or recognisable time period, geographical location or other world? This should be clear and will affect the direction, style of writing and possibly, the word-count.

PROTAGONIST (the main character) - every story needs a main character, i.e. the character whose point of view (PoV) is most prevalent and that your readers can become emotionally invested in.

GOAL - What is your protagonist trying to do? They need a goal, a wish, a desire or a need that makes the 'story'. This could be; escaping from a bad relationship, finding a lost treasure, discovering their true identity or, even simply getting through year five at school – but that goal should be clear because the reader needs to be rooting for them to succeed.

Week 1

OBSTACLES (or events) - Who or what is stopping, or making it difficult for the protagonist to achieve their goal? Obstacles can come from a single or multiple sources and can even be some aspect of the protagonists' character that becomes the obstacle. Without an obstacle, a story would not be much of a story.

The **RESOLUTION** - How does your protagonist achieve their goal, despite the obstacles? Perhaps they don't achieve their goal but, the resolution is their acceptance of this fact.

Five Finger Pitch Exercise 1

Pretty much every story can be summarised using the 'five finger pitch'.

📌 Test this theory out: consider a few books and/or films you have recently read or watched and see if you can identify your own answers to the following questions (in bold). Remember to think about the overall picture, rather than the specific details:

Film/Novel title: ET (science fiction film by Steven Spielberg)
Setting: Suburban California
Protagonist: the story is from the point of view of Elliot, the young boy who finds the alien.
Goal: Elliot is trying to get the alien (ET) back home
Obstacles: The government agencies who want to capture the alien
Satisfactory resolution: ET goes home

Film/Novel title: Harry Potter and the Philosopher's Stone
Setting: An ordinary English town and a magical 'parallel world'
Protagonist: Harry Potter
Goal: Trying to get through his first year at Wizarding School.
Obstacles: Having to stop Voldemort from getting the philosopher's stone.
Satisfactory resolution: Harry saves the stone and stops Voldemort.

Five Finger Pitch Exercise 2

You are going to use a Five Finger Pitch to plot and then write your own short story of around 500 words, using one of the improbable scenarios listed 1 to 5 below. Remember to describe what you see, how you feel and any smells, sounds or sensations you might experience too.

PROTAGONIST You are the main character.

GOAL You have an important meeting that you must attend, this afternoon – your future depends on it.

OBSTACLE (and SETTING) When I woke up this morning, I wasn't in my bedroom…..

Now select an **obstacle** from numbers 1 to 5 below. Randomise your selection by throwing a dice (create your own scenario if you throw a 6):

❶ …I was clinging to the branch of a tree, in a jungle full of dangerous creatures and poisonous plants.

❷ …My bed was a boat and I was in the middle of a choppy ocean, surrounded by sharks.

❸ …I was on the moon with a broken spacecraft and a rather angry alien.

❹ …I was trapped in a cage, hanging from the ceiling of a castle, surrounded by guards shouting, "Off with their head".

❺ …I was running through a network of underground tunnels, being chased by angry trolls.

RESOLUTION How will you get out of your predicament and arrive at your meeting on time?

Remember, this is your story and you can write your way out using absolutely any escape plan you can think of – be imaginative – crazy even – push yourself to be as daft and inventive as possible.

Week 1

Notes & ideas...

Week 1

Week 2

What does dialogue do?

- Dialogue adds 'voice' to a story
- Breaks up the monotony of the author's voice
- Can be used to move a story along
- Can show different points of view about a situation
- Allows the author to reveal more information about the characters

Authors are by nature, extremely interested in other people's conversations (to put it bluntly - we are nosey). When you listen in on conversations, especially in a coffee shop, pub, the school gate, etc.… you begin to realise that conversations have their own distinct genres (*categories/types*).

Here are some of my own silly suggestions for the conversation genres you are likely to hear, and I am sure you could think of a few more:

- Banal coffee-shop banter
- School-gate gossip
- Furtive-teenage whisperings
- Frantic-family yelling
- Couple-jousting
- Relationship-breakdown shouting
- Life and death level despair
- Angry strangers arguing
- One-sided romancing
- Romantic-duelling
- Steamy blush-inducing
- Old-time innuendo
- Information sharing
- Situation-controlling
- Evil/mal intent coercion
- Dastardly plotting

A quick note about writing authentic accents. Language is important for portraying regional and foreign accents. It can also denote age, social group, education, situation and mood, but when writing an accent, just use the bare minimum - less is most definitely more, or it will become too difficult to read.

Listen and take notes

Make a point of listening to the conversations going on around you and note the differences in the way people speak.

Make sure you listen to different age groups to get a feel for how differently they use language - particularly teenagers, who can sound like they are speaking in code. If you choose to write about teens, be aware that their slang-words and aspects of their language change more often than their socks and getting it wrong in your story can completely alienate them and invalidate your story, so – as with accents, use teen-speak sparingly.

Make notes about:

- Use of language – is it formal, casual or colloquial (*everyday*)?
- The speed at which different people speak
- What words are frequently repeated, and by whom?
- How do different (foreign and regional) accents make English words sound?
- Some people have unusual intonations or pitch uses (*the highs and lows of sentences*) – listen to where they occur in their sentences.
- Pay particular attention to the start of conversations, before the 'meaty' bit. Are there a random thoughts, half-sentences, niceties (*how are you, you're looking well, nice weather, etc…*).
- Can you 'categorise' the conversation genre (*as above*)?

Conversation Genre Exercise

🖋 **Write a short conversation between two characters** (*they can be made up or based on people you have listened to*) using one of the 'fun conversation genres' above. Try to give each character a consistent and authentic voice – in other words, use the sort of words and phrasing that character would use.

Week 2

Dialogue formatting recap

I have called this a recap because you probably already covered this in school, although some of the rules have relaxed a little as we become more 'Americanised' and publishers will have preferences which may differ from your usual use, depending on the audience and 'house style'.

UK versus USA: Should you use single or double speech (or quote) marks for speech? Well, it depends on which country you are writing in or for, and yours or your publisher's preferences. The main thing is to be consistent. If you use double quotes for direct speech (*dialogue*), you should then use single quotes for indirect speech (*quotes*). See what popular books in the genre you want to write in use.

- Use speech marks around the words each character speaks.

    "I'm going to the match," Juliette said. ⟵ The dialogue tag

- Begin a new paragraph each time a different person speaks - this makes it clear to the reader when the speaker has changed.

    "I hate football," said Emily.
    "Really? I can't understand why," said James.
    "It's a bunch of men kicking a bag of wind."
    "It's more exciting than shopping."

- When breaking a sentence with a dialogue tag, if the second part of dialogue is a continuation of the first sentence, use a comma after the dialogue tag and do not capitalize the first letter of the second piece of dialogue.

    "I can't help it," Jack said, "it's just the way I am."

    But if it is a new sentence (by the same person), use a full-stop after the dialogue tag and start the second sentence with a capital letter.

    "I don't know," Jack said. "By the way, how is your sister doing?"

- Dialogue should end with a full-stop (inside the speech marks) if it is the end of the line, or a comma if a dialogue tag follows.

    "That could be fun," said Frank.
    Jack shouted, "For goodness sake, do be quiet."

- When dialogue ends in a question or exclamation mark, dialogue tags that follow still start in lower case.

    "What's new?" she asked.

- If the dialogue ends with an ellipsis (…), you don't need to add any other punctuation.

    "If that's what you really want…" her voice faltering.

- If your character quotes someone else, then use single quotation marks. (Or vice-versa if using single quotes for the dialogue.)

    "But my mum specifically said, I must be 'IN THE HOUSE' by midnight, so I have to leave NOW."

Writing good dialogue

❶ **Avoid making characters tell each other things they already know.**

The example below will sound unrealistic and forced:

> "How long have we been married, Janet?"
> "Well, we got married in Toronto in 2010, so that's almost ten years."

You don't want the reader to know that you are using the dialogue to impart information, so you need to make the information-dumping more sneaky and less 'in your face'. For example, the important information you need your reader to know is that they married in Toronto, ten years ago, so make something of it and make sure it sounds authentic, so the reader doesn't feel like they are being 'informed'.

> "Ken and Helen are going to Toronto for their honeymoon – I think they're staying in that awful hotel next to the one we got married in."
> "Did you tell them it was a dump?"
> "I didn't have the heart – besides, that was over ten years ago, hopefully it's improved."

Dialogue Exercise 1

Two couples; Gita and Sunil, Arthur and Suzanne, are at a party together. Gita is a police officer and her husband writes crime thrillers, whilst working part-time as a solicitor. They have recently adopted Gita's twin nieces after her sister passed away. Arthur is an architect and he has two grown up children. Arthur and Suzanne are expecting their first child together and live part-time in France.

The reader does not yet know any of the above information.

✒ Write a short conversation between the characters to give the reader an insight into them.

You don't need to give all the information and you can include other characters. Do remember to SHOW not TELL.

Week 2

❷ **Don't enter a scene at the start of a conversation.**

Enter a conversation as late as you can because in written dialogue, you don't need the 'niceties' of normal conversation:

> *"Hi Jess, how are you?"*
> *"I'm good Sue, how are the kids?"*
> *"Oh, you know, it's all go in our house – did you ever get that patio finished?"*
> *"Not yet, we had a bit of an issue with it."*
> *"Oh, what was that?"*
> *"Well, we dug up a set of human bones – they're investigating them."*

The reader wants to get straight to the 'meat' of the conversation:

> Sue placed her coffee on the slightly sticky table, put her hands to her temples and took a deep breath.
> "Oh Jess, it's been horrible - Dave dug up the old patio and found remains."
> "Human remains?"
> "The police think so – they've taken over our entire garden."

It might feel like you are missing out vital parts of normal conversation – and you are, but think of it like this…. if you were listening in on a conversation (perhaps your parent's, when you were a child) at what point would your ears 'prick up' and start to take notice? That is the part your written dialogue should start at, so that you get your reader's attention and don't bore them.

Dialogue Exercise 2

Melanie bumps into a friend at the supermarket she hasn't seen for many years. Melanie married a billionaire, who has just been jailed on suspicion of serious fraud.

The reader does not yet know any of the above information.

> Write a short conversation between the two characters. Remember to dive straight into the interesting part of the conversation. You can write an opening paragraph to describe them meeting again for the first time and then get straight to the point.

Week 2

❸ **Use 'Action Beats' to enrich your dialogue.**

Action Beats are the short descriptions of action before, between or after dialogue. They can minimise or even negate the need for dialogue tags, whilst still making it clear who is speaking and also giving a sense of the characters' emotional state and the setting:

> *Alex steadied herself, placing a hand softly on Sam's cheek,* "They've found her."
> "And…?"
> "She's alive - just."
> "Oh, thank God." *Sam collapsed into Alex's arms.*

Using action beats instead of dialogue tags can also increase the pace of your dialogue, creating a sense of urgency, tension, or even panic.

Dialogue Exercise 3

Beatrice has been kidnapped, Tom is speaking to the police officer.

✎ Write the conversation between Tom and the Police officer as he explains what has happened to his daughter.

Use action beats to minimise your use of dialogue tags, to show the pace and urgency of the conversation and describe the emotional state of Tom and how the police officer reacts to him.

❹ **Always try to speak your dialogue aloud.**

Test your dialogue – if it is 'clunky', it will not flow and you will find it difficult to get the sentences out, or it might be repetitive, or worse still – boring.

If you have a willing friend (or friendly writing group), ask them to read your dialogue so that you can listen to it. This is important, because dialogue sounds entirely different when read aloud, than it does in your head.

Week 2

❺ Keep your dialogue tags simple.

'She said' or 'he said' is often perfectly adequate for denoting dialogue. Too many adverbs in dialogue tags (for example, *nervously, dejectedly, mournfully*) can distract from the actual speech. Instead, to infer how the words are spoken, you can use a character's actions to demonstrate their mood and emotion to the reader.

Rather than stating how the words are said:

> *"It's alright now," she whispered softly.*

You could infer the tone through her actions:

> *Sally bent down and tenderly pushed a stray hair from the child's ear, "It's alright now," she said.*

That's not to say you should not use different verbs and adverbs, such as 'she shrieked', 'he admonished', 'they wailed helplessly', etc… just don't over-use them – less is more powerful.

Dialogue Exercise 4

- Replace '*she wailed dejectedly*' in the dialogue below with '*she said*' and add a sentence to describe your character's mood, action or feelings to show the reader **how** Felicity says her dialogue instead.

  > *"I couldn't reach him," she wailed dejectedly.*

  Or create your own piece of dialogue with actions, instead of adverbs to denote how the words are delivered.

Week 2

❻ Use dialogue to reveal information about your characters.

You might need to tell your reader certain bits of information about your character's personality or characteristics – things that are necessary to the story, or to the reader's understanding of the character and their actions but, long sections of narrative can be off-putting and dull. A more interesting way to tell your reader about your character is to reveal that information through conversation.

For example, instead of telling your reader a character has had a limited education, you could make this clear through the things he says:

> "Do you want the spaghetti carbonara or the burger?" asked Joe.
> "I don't eat nothing I can't spell," said Jack.

What can you tell about Maria's life and how does Jean feel about it?

> "How can you stand to watch that tv show? It's so not like that!" Maria admonished.
> "Because some of us haven't ever lived the Californian dream," hissed Jean.

The family below are probably struggling for money, but resourceful.

> "Mum, you need to fix the zipper again, and the inside of the pocket has another hole."
> "Pop it on the side," said Martha, "I've got your dad's best socks to darn first."

Dialogue Exercise 5

✒ Write conversations between Emily and any other characters you wish to add in the situation detailed below. The dialogue should reveal that Emily is medically trained, but currently unemployed.

> Emily is in the same shop as Georgia, but does not know her. She sees Georgia become unwell.

Continue the story from the following sentence: *Georgia slumped against the shop counter, her legs went weak and she felt herself begin to fall...*

Week 2

Notes & ideas...

Week 2

Week 3

Point of View

Your protagonist is your reader's main point of reference and context from which they will understand your story – in other words, the reader will view your story from the protagonist's point of view – through their eyes. This is important, because your aim, when writing any story, will be to get the reader reading and to keep them reading to the end and this is done by having a character they can really get to know and hopefully become emotionally invested in.

Some authors use multiple character's points of view, but usually these are restricted to one per chapter or section and do not switch during that chapter or section.

Changing the point of view is like jumping in and out of different people's heads, which can be confusing for the reader (if not done well) and distract their interest away from the main character.

Third Person Point of View

A narrated story, referring to the main character using she, he and they pronouns.

This is the most common point of view in novels. Third Person PoV is also the easiest to write and there are two varieties:

- Third Person PoV **Omniscient** - the narrator (author) tells the story from many perspectives because they know the thoughts and feelings of all the characters in the story.

- Third Person PoV **Limited** – similar to First Person, but more detached, the narrator tells the story from the perspective of only the main character.

First Person Point of View

The main character is the narrator, using I, we and me pronouns.

The main character tells the story to the reader. This makes it trickier for the author to show what other characters get up to, unless the main character actually witnesses or hears about them. It does however, lend a great deal of intimacy to the story because you are seeing things directly through the eyes of the narrator/main character.

Here is an example from my novel 'Crime and Cremation':

> *"It's fine, the fuse is always blowing, it happened to me, like, three times last week," I lie.*
> *Then we both hear the noise, but this time it is coming from my dad's study. Bloody cat! I grab one of Mum's candles, the one she thinks is far too pretty to use and casually light it.*

Second Person Point of View

The reader is the main character, using the pronouns you!

You are the main character in the story – although the author is telling you what you did and thought. Very few novels are written in second person because it is extremely difficult to do well and from a reader's point of view, it almost feels like you are being 'directed' in a play.

Below is an example of second person narrative:

> *You open the door, expecting it to be your withering mother, but no, you find yourself face-to-face with a scarlet-faced teenager. Holding a gun.*
> *You don't know what to do, and the split second you take to consider your options proves to be the undoing of you.*

Week 3

Point of View Exercise 1

Liam is stuck on a train. He had to work late again because it is the only way to keep on top of his work-load and ensure he meets his deadlines. He has two younger executives snapping at his heels for his job; which is precarious under the latest management re-shuffle.

The train that Liam is on is Southern Rail – so it is indefinitely delayed. He promised to help his wife Lisa move the bed around in the spare room so that her parents could come and stay next week. There is no phone signal to call Lisa to let her know he is on his way home and he forgot to call her before he left the office. It is 9.45pm.

📌 Write a couple of paragraphs on Liam's frustration from his own perspective, using **First Person PoV**.

For example: *My stress levels were already soaring, after my run-in with the boss and then I was on a train, going nowhere with no way to let Lisa know I was running late – she was going to kill me…*

Point of View Exercise 2

Lisa is beginning to wonder if her husband (Liam, *above*) is having an affair. She is a busy school teacher in a tiny village school and she doesn't get out of their village very often, so she has very little understanding of commuting and working in a business environment.

📌 Write a couple of paragraphs about Lisa's worries, from her own perspective, using **Third Person PoV**.

For example: *Lisa kept checking her messages, but there was nothing from Liam, where could he be, she wondered…*

Week 3

A 'baddie's point of view

A reader will be sympathetic to a victim – they can relate to or at least understand their anguish and will generally want to root for them. It is harder to invest your precious reading time on a character you despise or cannot relate to in any way.

If you write from the point of view of the 'baddie', then you will need to give them some likeable, or at the very least, relatable characteristics. It may be that they have a deeper purpose that is essentially moralistic or good, or a backstory that explains their actions and allows the reader to sympathise with them.

If they are the main protagonist of the story, you need to give your reader something to 'buy into' – a reason to want to follow their story.

- A film example of this is the Robin, Prince of Thieves movie, starring Kevin Costner. The baddie, played by Alan Rickman was evil and despicable and yet he is a much loved character. Why? Possibly because we were shown his backstory – a hint at the awful childhood he must have had with a wicked witch for a mother – suddenly, we can see why he is the way he is and we have empathy.

- Another example is the Karate Kid – this is an unusual situation, in that the Bully and the Victim were clearly defined in the film and yet, fans of the movie point out that in reality, the Victim was actually bullying the Bully and that the Bully was, at many times, actually the Victim BUT because it was filmed from the PoV of the Victim (the Karate Kid), we only see it from one side. Interestingly a TV series, following the original characters as adults, takes this on board and is filmed from two separate and equal points of view. Of course, this can also work in a book.

Point of View Exercise 3

- Write a 500 word story from the perspective of a 'baddie'. What characteristics will endear them to the reader? Perhaps the 'victim' can be a pain in the neck and thoroughly unlikeable. Use First or Third person point of view.

Week 3

Character Profiles

Stories often feature characters who are clearly good, or blatantly bad but, if this was their only attribute, they would be 'flat' and uninteresting. People are complex and even the best people have negative points and vice-versa.

A 'GOOD' CHARACTER

Name: Alicia Bento

Description:
Age, appearance, habits… Tall, mixed race – Japanese and English. Dark, shoulder-length hair. Quietly spoken and smiles a lot. Should wear glasses, but doesn't, consequently squints when trying to read anything.

Job: Trainee architect

Hobbies: Wind-surfing, reading and salsa dancing

☑ Positive: Friendly and open to everyone

☑ Positive: Helps her single sister with her children

☑ Positive: Always very punctual and reliable

☑ Positive: Really good cook

☒ Negative: Gets flustered easily

☒ Negative: Atrociously bad driver

A 'BAD' CHARACTER

Name: Georgina Larson

Description: (Age, appearance, habits...) Tiny, Welsh, Long-blonde hair, very beautiful. Loud voice. Forever flicking her hair out of her eyes.

Job: Children's tennis coach

Hobbies: All sports and mountain climbing. Partying

☒ **Negative:** Likes to argue with everyone

☒ **Negative:** Very vain

☒ **Negative:** Opinionated and unfiltered

☒ **Negative:** Lazy with anything she doesn't fancy doing

☑ **Positive:** Is an excellent tennis coach

☑ **Positive:** Is really kind and helpful to her elderly neighbour

Keep your character profiles to hand when you are writing longer pieces, so you are consistent in your treatment of them. They don't need to be specifically labelled as 'good' or 'bad', unless you want to.

You can do Character Profile sheets for all the characters in your story, or just the main ones – it is up to you. Some writing software even lets you create these within their system, but a notebook or folder is perfectly adequate too.

A useful way to keep your main characters in mind, is to find an image on the internet of someone who looks like you imagine your character would, print it out and stick it to your character profile page, or on a pin-board above where you write.

Week 3

Character profile Exercise 1

✒ Create character profiles for up to five characters. Try to select a range of ages, ethnicities. They can be all good, all bad or a mix – it is up to you.

Character profile Exercise 2

✒ Use your character profiles to create a story of up to 1500 words, where your five characters are brought together in an unusual location or circumstance, for example; a desert island ship-wreck, the funeral of a mutual friend, a puppy-training class, or a disaster at a theme-park.

Refer to your profile sheets so that you are consistent with your characters' traits and how they might interact with each other in the story.

➲ Which one will be the main character? This is the person whose perspective we see the story from.

Notes & ideas...

Week 3

Week 4

Tenses

When writing a story, there are two tense options; **present tense** and **past tense**.

The majority of novels are written in past tense – as in, the action is being recounted after the event. This is a 'comfortable' tense to both read and write.

A novel written in Present Tense is happening RIGHT NOW and has a number of pros and cons, which should be considered when using it.

Past Tense example:

The car smelled fusty from the camping gear. I did up my seatbelt and took a deep breath, "This is it, freedom," I told myself.

A week away, no kids, no work and no commitments. I did a final check; tent, sleeping bag, food…

The kids looked glum, but I was sure they would survive their week with Grandma. Slowly, trying not to seem too eager, I put the car into gear and drove away.

Present Tense example (using the same scene):

The car smells slightly damp, I think the camping gear must be a bit fusty - oh well. I click my seatbelt shut and take a deep breath.

"This is it, freedom," I tell myself.

I do a final check; tent, sleeping bag, food… wave goodbye to mum and the kids, trying not to acknowledge Lauren and Toby's glum faces. They'll survive a week with Grandma…

I jam the car into gear and try not to look too eager as I pull away.

Consider carefully about whether present tense is the best choice for your story:

The positive aspects of Present Tense

- Present tense can feel like a movie
- Present tense intensifies your connection with character's emotions
- Present tense works best in short-time-frame stories with constant action

Negative aspects of Present Tense:

- Some readers positively HATE present tense
- Present tense is less flexible because time shifts can be awkward
- Present tense tricky to write well and easy to get wrong
- There is less narration and often, lots of dialogue.

Future tense is a 'thing', but difficult to keep up for any writing of length.

Future Tense example (using the same scene):

The car will smell damp from the fusty camping gear. I will have to check I have all my equipment; the tent, sleeping bag, food…

I shall acknowledge my freedom and try not to be affected by the glum faces of my children, who will have a great time with grandma.

Then I will drive off slowly, so as not to seem too excited to be free of them for the week.

Tenses Exercise 1

📌 Using **past** tense, write a description of a journey that you have already taken.

Use past tense verbs, for example; did, had, ran, saw, watched.

Tenses Exercise 2

📌 Using **present** tense, write a description of that same journey, as if you are actually taking it now.

Be very careful to make sure all your verbs are in the present tense - for example; do, have, run, see, watch.

Tenses Exercise 3

📌 Using **present** tense, write a short story about a character who has just discovered a hidden cave, whilst on a beach in Cornwall.

How do they discover the cave and what is inside it? Don't forget to describe any smells, sounds or feelings your character experiences.

AND IF YOU REALLY HATE PRESENT TENSE.

Do the same exercise using **Past** tense – it's absolutely fine. Focus on describing how your character feels and what they observe.

Writing Pace

Think about the pace of action in movies. It often moves slowly in a love story, frantically in a thriller, jumps about in a comedy and can be staccato in a horror. You can replicate the same 'feeling of pace' with your writing, by changing the lengths of your sentences and therefore the speed and smoothness of your delivery.

Short sentences

- Short sentences can signify that something may be about to happen and can create the necessary tension leading up the 'happening'.

    For example:

    The night was clear. She could see the road ahead. Nothing to worry about. Nothing at all.

- A series of super-short sentences can draw the reader's attention to details of significance.

    For example:

    "She meandered down along Oxford Street. Long hair bouncing, non-descript yoga-pants and well-used gym bag. The only detail giving away her status was her watch. Patek Philippe. Calatrava. Alligator strap. Rose gold case. About eighteen thousand pounds."

    In the above example, short sentences are used to depict the features of a particular detail; the expensive watch. The writer has drawn our attention to it for a reason.

- Short, sharp sentences are great for action scenes where there is lots going on simultaneously. You want to provide the reader with 'glimpses' of every bit of action in a 'gun-fire' manner.

    Jack led them in. Guns fire incessantly. All exits blocked. Troops surrounded them. More explosions. Blood. Pitiful cries. No hope.

Long sentences

- Long sentences are used to develop a slow-burning build-up of tension, unlike short sentence, which bring immediate tension.
- For 'painting' vivid descriptions that draw the reader in, particularly depicting nature, or romantic scenes.

From some points of view, long sentences have become 'old fashioned' and boring – this may well be true in many teen/YA novels and 'chic lit'. I believe this stems from our modern, time-starved, social media-driven lives, in which we only ever read 'snippets' of information and many people have lost the will and ability to hold their attention on longer pieces of writing (indeed there is an app that will condense a book into a mere fifteen minutes of key points).

This does not mean you shouldn't use beautifully constructed, long sentences BUT, that you should have an awareness of the modern reader and the market you are aiming your writing at.

Vary your sentence length.

Imagine your reader is floating down a river – sometimes they are meandering through beautiful scenery and having a lovely relaxing time, then occasionally, they drop into a death-defying rapid, or slide into a patch of choppy water. If you really want to wake your reader up, you can suddenly throw them down a waterfall – metaphorically speaking, of course.

Pace Exercise 1

- Your character is being chased through a woodland by a man she does not know, write two different versions of the same scene:

  1. **First person** PoV (I, me, we), short punchy sentences
  2. **Third person** PoV (she, he, they), with longer, descriptive sentences

Read each scene back, or ask a friend to read them for you. How does the sentence length and PoV affect the scene?

Pace Exercise 2

🖈 Write a short scene where a main character is waiting to meet someone.

Are they nervous, excited, fearful or angry? Use sentence length to show the feelings of your character in anticipation of this meeting but, don't tell the reader who they are meeting with – the descriptions should give an indication.

For example – short sentences:

She waited. Walked on the spot to warm her feet. He should be here. He promised he would. Wished she had said no. Footsteps. Too late, he was coming. Heart-beat quickened. Too late to leave now.

For example – long sentences:

She watched patiently, as swathes of commuters, coffee in hand, rushed and brushed past her. It had been nearly thirty-minutes and she was on the verge of leaving, but the thought of seeing him one more time, if only to answer her questions, had kept her glued to the rendezvous point. She caught her breath as she heard a familiar footfall, distinctly audible above the crowd, steadily approaching from behind.

Notes & ideas...

Week 4

Week 5

Literary devices are the techniques you can apply to your writing to control or direct how your reader feels when they read your story. Remember, each time you write a story, you are taking your reader on a journey into the life and mind of your characters – you want them to experience it as you see it and you do this with your writing, so the more techniques you can master, the more you can 'play God' with the emotions of your reader.

Poetic devices

These 'poetic' devices can be equally utilised in prose to evoke a more 'romanticised' or 'painterly' feeling to a description.

Alliteration is the occurrence of the same letter or sound at the beginning of adjacent or closely connected words, such as in; *Silly Susan sat silently sizzling sausages.*

Or more subtly;

> **C**louds **c**rowded over the **c**ornfield to form **s**waying **s**hadows that rattled ominously in the gathering breeze.

Assonance is like alliteration but, refers to the vowel sounds between syllables of nearby words.

> *He leaned where the old brick wall had been, falling backwards into the chilly stream. Nancy laughed and reminded herself to make a sign.*

Consonance: the recurrence of similar-sounding consonants in close proximity (but not necessarily at the beginning of all the words, because that would be alliteration!)

> *Caugh**t** in s**t**a**t**ic con**t**empla**t**ion.* (A repetition of the 'c' and 't' sounds)

The use of any of these 'matching sound' devices can give your sentences an ethereal/dreamy quality, which is particularly good for romantic scenes, descriptions of faraway places and reminiscences.

All of these AND rhyming are also particularly effective when writing for younger children because of the way these sounds 'roll around the mouth'. For example, everyone has at some point, enjoyed alliterative rhymes such as *'seven sizzling sausages'* and *'she sells seashells beside the seashore'*. Of course, in writing for adults, the trick is to use these devices in a way that is NOT obvious and does not 'jar' the reader, but simply enhances the flow of the sentence.

Poetic devices Exercise

- Describe an amazing setting – it can be a real or imaginary place. Use 'poetic' devices like assonance, consonance or alliteration to bring the wonder of the place to life.

  Read it back to yourself and make sure that any poetic devices are subtle. You do not want them to sound 'laboured' or over-done.

Avoid repetition of words, except…

If you use the same word several times, in close proximity to each other, it will really stand out to the reader and feel laboured. Always check your writing for repeats and if possible, change second and third repetitions of a word to a different one with the same meaning.

> *Malone had parked her car in the <u>car park</u> and taken the lift down to the shopping precinct. She felt nervous on her first trip out alone and had <u>nervously</u> looked over her shoulder several times on the way from her <u>car</u> to the <u>precinct</u>.*

Use a thesaurus to find good alternative words; MS Word's inbuilt Thesaurus (*select the word you want to change and press* **SHIFT** *and* **F7**), download a Thesaurus app for your smartphone or Google 'Thesaurus' for an online version.

Malone had parked her car in the multi-story and taken the lift down to the shopping precinct. She felt nervous on her first trip out alone and had <u>anxiously</u> looked over her shoulder several times on the way from her vehicle to the shops.

However…. a word **can** actually **be repeated** as a literary device – to reiterate a feeling or a sense and to build tension.

The night was clear. She could see the road ahead. Nothing to worry about. Nothing at all.

The repetition of the word 'Nothing' actually makes you feel the opposite – that perhaps there **is** something to worry about and puts you/the reader on edge.

Repetition can also be used as a stylistic device.

For example:

Gail did not know what was coming. She didn't know what was coming until it was too late to run…

The trick is, to make conscious decisions about the words and repetitions you use.

Repetitions Exercise

📌 Write a paragraph or two for the scenario below, using repetition to make the reader doubt that the young girl is as safe as she believes herself to be:

Celeste is fifteen. She is meeting a man she connected with on Tinder (a dating app). He says he is looking for teenagers to test out a new dating app designed for under eighteens.

Notes & ideas...

Week 5

Week 6

Launch into Poetry

One of the most difficult aspects of writing poetry (or indeed anything!) is coming up with a topic or theme. The following exercise is a fun way to create a poem using inspiration from other people's words.

Found Words Poetry Exercise

The purpose of this exercise is to use words or phrases that you might not have thought of before, therefore expanding your word repertoire and creating a poem with a theme or subject you may not have previously considered.

Take a selection of books, magazines, technical books – as random as possible. Perhaps do this at the library and delve into sections you might not normally use, such as scientific books, philosophy or even car manuals!

Open each book at any page and select words and phrases that you like the sound of. Don't select to a theme, be completely random and write the words/phrases down from different sources, until you have about twenty in total.

Now, choose the ones you like best (or use all of them if you like) to create your poem. The poem can be any style and you can add your own words around the 'found' words and phrases, or just use what you found.

Below is an example of one that I wrote whilst on a poetry workshop doing this very exercise. You can probably tell that most of my preferred phrases came from a magazine with an article about climate change! I added my own words to the found words in this example.

DROUGHT
A 'found words' poem

Penetrate the meniscus
Press a finger through and
Feel the silent WHOOSH
As water greedily
Devours your digit
Fractured blues and hues
Of turquoise puzzle-pieces
Slap and lap and try
To tie you up in weedy knots
Of liquid treachery
A trillion gallons of
Dew and thawing permafrost
Curate their murky ambition
With pharmaceutical fish
Pump the aquifer dry
For supreme magic to purify
The climate-science circles
Of tepid doubts on drought

What you might notice in this poem, is the use of alliteration, assonance and consonance, I discussed in week 5.

Penetrate the meniscus
Press a finger through and
Feel the silent WHOOSH
As water greedily
Devours your digit
Fractured blues and hues
Of turquoise puzzle-pieces
Slap and lap and try
To tie you up in weedy knots
Of liquid treachery
A trillion gallons of
Dew and thawing permafrost
Curate their murky ambition
With pharmaceutical fish
Pump the aquifer dry
For supreme magic to purify
The climate-science circles
Of tepid doubts on drought

Although it can appear that the repetition of letter sounds is purely accidental in a poem, often this is not the case and the poet will have worked hard to create the matching sounds that are so pleasing to the ear and enjoyable to the mouth when reading it aloud.

Notes & ideas...

Week 6

Week 7

What turns words into poetry?

How does a poem differ from ordinary prose? Poems with rhyming lines and obvious rhythm are easy to recognise, but words can still be a poem without these elements.

For me, it is in the moulding of the words. A poem that has had work done to it – like a lump of clay that is roughly formed into the shape of a vase and then painstakingly worked on until it is perfect, lovingly fired and adorned with colour.

I recommend you visit the websites below to read different types of poems and to also hear them being read aloud (Poetry Foundation). Poems are designed to be heard – they often make more sense when they are read aloud; indeed, learning how to read poetry is a skill in itself and if you get a chance to go to an 'open mic poetry night', you will probably hear the marked difference between poets who simply read their poems out loud and those who 'perform' them.

www.poetryfoundation.org/learn

www.writersdigest.com/whats-new/list-of-50-poetic-forms-for-poets

The (optional) ingredients of a poem

- **A message or a story.** A poem often has a message; be it political, personal or satirical. Or it can be a story, a moral, or an observation.

  Two examples of poems that tell stories are *Annabel Lee* by Edgar Allan Poe and *Madeline* by Ludwig Bemelmans.

  Lots of poems for children contain morals. A slightly gruesome example is *Matilda* by Hilaire Belloc which explains the importance of telling the truth.

- **Form or structure.** Poems often have a form; a set structure, such as rhyming pairs of lines, or a specific rhyme scheme, a pattern of repeating lines, a set number of syllables per line and a specific line count for each stanza (verse). Sometimes they have an actual physical shape (a concrete poem), like a Christmas tree, or anything really.

```
            A
         Concrete
      Poem is shaped on
      The page, like this one
    In the guise of a plump little
  Christmas tree, merry and bright
            For
            You
```

> *Quick reminder:*
> A syllable is a part of a word that has a single vowel sound and is said as a single unit - for example, TREE has only one syllable, FALLING has two FALL-ING, INTERNAL has three IN-TER-NAL and INSTITUTIONAL has five IN-STI-TU-TION-AL.

- **Rhyme scheme (or none).** Many popular poems rhyme, but the taste for rhyming comes and goes and currently, it is out of fashion. However, the reason many poems remain popular is **because** of their memorable and pleasing rhymes.

- **Rhythm.** Like a song with a defining drum beat, many poems have a rhythm that is intentionally set by writer. The most well-known of these is the IAMBIC PENTAMETER, used by Shakespeare; which is the use of alternating stressed and unstressed syllables that make the poem lines read with a 'da-dum, da-dum, da-um, da-dum, da-dum beat. This the first (and probably, most famous) line from William Shakespeare's Sonnet 18, showing the stressed syllables in bold:

*Shall **I** com**pare** thee **to** a **sum**mer's day?*

- **Style.** The style, or 'voice' of a poem will often match the subject - unusual 'turns of phrase' can be used, as well as made-up words strange pronunciations and all sorts. You can really mess around with language in a poem.

- **Punctuation and Line breaks.** In a poem, a sentence can be broken up into several lines – even mid-sentence to make it fit the 'form' or chosen rhyme-scheme. A line break can also work as punctuation, because the reader will naturally pause at the end of a line (unless you direct them not to, when it is performed).

    For example, in this poem extract from my production, The Death and Life of the Hippodrome, one sentence is broken into four lines, to force it to fit the eleven syllables per-line form that I chose:

    > *It was commonly known that sailors in need*
    > *Of earning some money, were sure to succeed*
    > *To gain a small income from pulling the ropes*
    > *At local playhouses, not far from their boats*

    However, when this poem is performed, it is read as one sentence:

    > *It was commonly known that sailors in need of earning some money were sure to succeed, to gain a small income from pulling the ropes at local playhouses, not far from their boats.*

    Some poems have punctuation (commas, full-stops, etc...), some have none. In modern poetry, either is fine. The key is to ensure the reader understands how to read the poem through the writer's use of either line-breaks, punctuation, or a combination of both

- **Or none.** A poem may have none of the above ingredients.

    Free verse has little to differentiate itself from prose – however, it is the intention of the writer and the work done to the words that define it as a poem (in my personal opinion), although not everyone is a fan, or would agree with this!

Poem forms

There are all sorts of rhyme schemes used in poetry and these are denoted by letter patterns, showing which lines rhyme with which, for example: alternate rhyming lines are an ABAB rhyme scheme, like in this extract from my poem called Pelt:

> A fox of **notoriety** (**A**)
> A tail of thick and fiery **fur** (**B**)
> Producer of strong **progeny** (**A**)
> Sly master of the bin **procure** (**B**)

Rhyming couplets (pairs of rhyming lines) are AA, BB, CC and so on, seen here in my poem, Night.

> Day turns to night and then night slinks **away** (**A**)
> Overawed by her aura, embarrassed to **stay** (**A**)
> She reproaches his tricks and his childish **pranks** (**B**)
> And the nightmare conspirators caught in his **ranks** (**B**)
> The streetlights abetting his fingering **shadows** (**C**)
> The devious rustlings of ravenous **hedgerows** (**C**)

Mix these patterns with FORM and set SYLLABLE COUNTS and other rules, and poetry can become quite complex (but extremely fun) to write!

Some common poetic forms (there are lots more)

> Quick reminder: a stanza is a set of lines in a poem with a set form. A verse is pretty much the same thing but refers to sets of lines in a poem without a form.

Acrostic: This is a very popular form for children to write because the only rule is that when you read the first letter of each line in the poem, going downwards, it will spell out a word or a message. Obviously, you need to choose the word or message before you write the poem.

Triplet: Uses rhyme scheme in sets of AAA.

Monorhyme: Is a poem in which every line ends with the same rhyme sound.

Enclosed rhyme: Uses rhyme scheme of ABBA for each stanza. Which means that the first and fourth lines rhyme, and the two middle lines rhyme.

Terza rima: Uses an unlimited number of stanzas of three lines each (called tercets) and has rhyme pattern of ABA BCB CDC DED, which means that the middle line of each stanza becomes the first and third line rhymes for the next stanza. A Terza rima usually ends with either a single line, or a rhyming couplet using the same rhyme sound as the middle line from the previous (last) stanza or tercet.

Limerick: Is usually a humorous (and sometimes rude) poem, quite often poking fun at someone or something. It is only five lines long and has a rhyme scheme of AABBA.

Villanelle: A nineteen-line poem consisting of five tercets (*stanzas of three lines each*) and a final quatrain (*four line stanza*).

It uses a rhyme scheme of A1bA2, abA1, abA2, abA1, abA2, abA1A2. The number denotes a repeating line, in that line one (A1) is repeated in line six, twelve and eighteen, then line three (A2) is also repeated at lines nine, fifteen and nineteen.

So, although this sounds very complicated, there are two lines that are repeated four times each – so that's eight lines dealt with, then there are eleven unique lines – one in the first stanza, then two in each of the subsequent stanzas.

A good example of this poem is '*Do Not Go Gentle Into That Good Night*' by Dylan Thomas, which you can easily find if you search for it online.

Haiku: Is a non-rhyming, three line poem, where first and last lines have five syllables, and the middle has seven syllables. It is an Anglicized version of a traditional Japanese form and the subject is often nature or the seasons and the third line is a 'cutting line' that juxtaposes (contrasts with) the previous two.

These are two examples of my own Haiku:

Kitchen in silence
Only dishes scream loudly
The eating is done

Puberty looms in
The spring between seasons where
Tributaries swell.

Week 7

Triolet: For a short poem, a Triolet has an awful lot of rules! It is a bit like a short Villanelle.

It has eight lines in two stanzas of four lines each but, only five lines that are different. Line one is repeated as lines four and seven. Line two is also the last line. The rhyming pattern is A1BaA1 abA1B1, where the capital letters are the repeating lines. Here's one of mine, called Tiger:

> You tear at my skin with piercing words (**A1**)
> And I bleed just a little for you (**B1**)
> Reassemble myself with the view you preferred (**a**)
> You tear at my skin with piercing words (**A1**)
>
> And my acid retort is unheard (**a**)
> As I observe my existence undo (**b**)
> You tear at my skin with piercing words (**A1**)
> And I bleed just a little for you (**B1**)

One way to approach writing a triolet (if you fancy it), is to write the last line first, because this is the line that holds the IMPACT of the poem. Then write the line that goes before it and you'll only have three unique lines left to write.

Free verse: has no rules. You can do what you want with it. Here's one of mine, called The Awful Dilemma of Parenting:

> A decision is made, or made for you, or made without your knowledge
> But somehow, anyhow, your child is here, NOW, waiting for guidance
> And whether you stumbled into parenthood or not
> Each choice you make from this point forward
> Directs the future of your progeny, their progeny
> And your genes beyond
> A significant slice of humanity, for a hundred years to come
> Affected by the quality of your parenting skills.
> Suddenly, the gravity of fish-fingers
> Weigh concrete on your mind

Rondeau: fifteen lines, octosyllabic (eight syllables per line), A1ABBA- AABA1 –AABBA1, although I cheated a little; because the repeating line at lines nine and fifteen should only be the first four syllables of line one. I guess that's what you call *poetic licence!*

Look up the much-loved Rondeau 'In Flanders Fields' by John McCrea. Here is my own example of a Rondeau, called The Harbinger of Glottenham:

> The coming of a speeding coach (**A1**)
> A squid-ink-black soundless approach (**A**)
> Hidden hop-pickers bathed in sweat (**B**)
> Ignore the horror's swift beset (**B**)
> The Castle's future days approach (**A**)
>
> The Lady's envoi braves to broach (**A**)
> So slogs his legs up Glotte'nham's slope (**A**)
> To tell his mistress he regrets (**B**)
> The coming of the speeding coach (**A1**)
>
> As sliding planes of time encroach (**A**)
> The Lady paces round her moat (**A**)
> Her ghostly spectre paid her debt (**B**)
> And now another's time is set (**B**)
> The harbinger who brings no hope (**A**)
> The coming of death's speeding coach. (**A1**)

Poetry Exercise 1

🖋 Choose a poetic form from above, or search for 'poetic forms' online and choose one to write your own poem. I know a lot of poets HATE writing under such restrictions, BUT I really recommend you have a go, because writing to a strict set of rules actually forces you to think more creatively in order to find the right words to tell your story or voice your message.

Poetic clichés

> A phrase or opinion that is overused and betrays a lack of original thought.

It is very easy to use clichés in poetry, such as 'as soft as a feather', 'only time will tell', 'fall head over heels' and so on. Finding original ways to describe things can be tricky, but there are techniques to get yourself out of the poetic rut.

Try the exercise below to come up with some unusual phrase combinations.

Note: When I do this exercise with kids' groups, I get the children to lie on the ground outside, to get a different perspective on the world.

Poetry Exercise 2

This is best done outside, but could be done inside, or even by looking online.

Nouns: find and list five objects, big or small, singular or plural (*preferably a mix of both*). Complete this column first, then complete the next columns.

Verbs: find and list five things that move (*a mix of mechanical and organic*) and next to each one, write a verb that describes its movement.

Adjectives: listen to the sounds around you and list five them with an adjective that describes each sound.

Nouns	Verbs	Adjectives
Stones	(*traffic lights*) change	(*bird sings*) mournfully
Pond	(*leaves*) flutter	(*airplane flies*) noiselessly
Lovers	(*tractor*) trundles	(*trees bend*) angrily
Car	(*dogs*) dart	(*church bell rings*) ominously
Sheep	(*gramophone*) spirals	(*bee buzzes*) industriously

Now try out some of the noun-verb-adjective phrase combinations and see if you can find any that could work in a poem. In my example, I liked *'sheep trundle mournfully'*, *'lovers change angrily'*, *'stones spiral ominously'*, *'cars dart industriously* and *'pond spirals noiselessly'*. You can add or remove 's' on the end of words where necessary.

Week 7

Poetry Exercise 3

We often use colour in our writing, both in poetry and prose and it is one area where a bit of imagination can really 'lift' your writing and avoid more dreaded clichés.

📌 Take the list of colours below and add more of your own, then go onto the internet and search through images in that colour (Google 'things that are yellow' under IMAGES), listing the most unusual or obscure ones you can find.

Colour	Cliché	Alternatives
Yellow	Daffodil, sunset	Cheese, rain hat, submarine
Blue	Lake, sky	Cheese vein, corpse lips
Green	Grass	Thallium flame, party, coriander
Orange	Tango	Muppet, fish batter
Turquoise	Tropical sea	Bread mould, Cornish pottery
Black	Squid ink, night sky	Top hat, 7 inch (or 12 inch)

Some examples using my colour alternatives above:

Her eyes were the colour of Cornish pottery and her hair a Muppet orange.

The Northern Lights turned the sky into thallium flames.

The sea spun around them, shining black as 12 inch record.

Notes & ideas...

Week 7

Week 8

Theme

A theme is a unifying idea that is developed throughout a story. It differs from the subject of the story and is the subtle message or underlying issue you wish to convey to your reader, without seeming to 'preach'.

It is common in stories for children is to have a moralistic theme.

Teenage and YA (*Young Adult*) books often have Romance, Friendship or Teenage Angst as the theme, although lately, Surviving Mental Health and Living with a Chronic Illness have also featured.

Chick Lit generally has Finding True Love as the theme

Other common themes are: space, relationships, power and control, friendship, adventure, conflict, betrayal…

Sometimes a theme reveals itself.

You don't necessarily have to write with a theme in mind when start your first draft. Re-reading your story for the first time, may reveal its point (theme), if you didn't write with one in mind. It could be something unexpected – a subconscious idea that you hadn't managed to clarify, but somehow came out in your narrative (it happens!). Your job then is to strengthen the theme using subtle hints in characterisation and dialogue, so that the narrative hangs together. On the other hand, if theme is too obvious, it may need toning down so that it fades into the background.

Do not confuse Theme with Genre.

Genre

Genre is the commercial category your story fits within and often defines the style, length and to a degree, the language or writing style used.

A reader will often have a preference for a particular genre of book and will have certain expectations of it. If an author steps too far away from the expected norms of that genre – for example, if Paranormal Romance fails to have any spookiness to it, or if a Chick Lit novel doesn't supply a happy ending, then many of its readers will be disappointed.

Some common genres are:

Classic genres:	Major genres:	Newer Genres:
Tragedy	Science fiction	Fan fiction
Tragic comedy	Crime	LGBT Erotica
Fantasy	Drama	Speculative fiction
Mythology	Romance	Dystopian
Adventure	Action / Adventure	Cozy mystery
Mystery	Satire / Dark humour	
	Horror	

These are certainly not the only categories – there are loads more.

When you browse for a book on Amazon, you will see the genre categories listed on the left hand side of the screen (*and sometimes across the top of the page*).

There are categories and sub-categories of genre and the lists are extensive. Here is an example of the sub-categories under **Crime, Thrillers & Mystery**:

Action & Adventure	Medical	Sherlock Holmes
Anthologies	Mystery	Short Stories
British Detectives	Police Procedurals	Spy Stories
Hard-Boiled	Political	Technothrillers
Historical	Psychological	Thrillers
Legal	Series	Women Sleuths

When you write a short story or a novel, it is worth being familiar with the genre you are planning to writing in – take a look at other books within that genre, even if you just look them up on Amazon and read the back cover (*sometimes* books will have a 'Look inside' feature which allows you to read the first few pages).

Theme and Genre Exercise

- Think of some books you have recently read and see if you can work what their themes and genre are.

For example:

Harry Potter sits in the Fantasy genres. According to the author, one of its main themes is Death. Other themes prevalent throughout the series are; Good v Evil, Friendship and Love.

My novella, **Crime and Cremation** is in the Crime and Dark Humour genres. The theme is - *How far can good morals stretch?*

My teen novel, **FREEN: The First Truth** is in the YA and Science Fiction genres. The theme was - *Do people really want to know the truth?*

New Genre Exercise

We tend to stick with what we know, and indeed, the recommended advice is to write what you know BUT, if you don't try writing in different, less comfortable genres, how will you ever know if they might suite you really well.

- Take a deep breath and pick a genre from the following list – one that you have never tried before – perhaps one that really scares you, and write a 500 word story in it. Try several, if you fancy it.

Gothic

Romanticised horror (or death or mystery) popularised in the Victorian era. Lots of skirting around the issue using flowery, overly-dramatic, romantic language set against a bleak and haunting backdrop. Lots of internal thoughts of monologues.

(*The Castle of Otranto by Horace Walpole - 1764, Wuthering Heights by Emily Brontë - 1847, The Picture of Dorian Gray by Oscar Wilde - 1890, Dracula by Bram Stoker – 1897*)

Science Fiction

Hi-tech new worlds, new technology, new science, new structure and lots of terminology including new ways to travel. Can be set on earth or on another planet, or even in another dimension.

(*1984 by George Orwell, Altered Carbon by Richard K. Morgan, Brave New World by Aldous Huxley, Dune by Frank Herbert, Watchers by Dean Koontz*)

Fantasy

Complex new world orders in fictional worlds - frequently medieval in style. Fantastical characters, usually in complex hierarchies. Often inspired by folk stories and myths. Magic or supernatural events. New ways of doing things.

(*Harry Potter series by J.K Rowling, Game of Thrones by George R.R Martin, Moon Called by Patricia Briggs, Thief of Time by Terry Pratchett, Cloud Atlas by David Mitchell*)

Horror

A story that builds on the reader's sense of fear. Usually begins in a happy, normal place then builds to knife-edge suspense culminating in horrific events. Atmosphere and sense of emotional dread. Tense moments that amount to nothing and other people not believing there is anything untoward going on, although there is often a character who does know and gives hints or warns off the main character. Does not necessarily need to contain lots of blood, gore and death.

(*Bird Box by Josh Malerman, Interview With the Vampire by Anne Rice, The Silence of the Lambs by Thomas Harris, Pet Sematary by Stephen King, Rosemary's Baby by Ira Levin*)

Dystopian

Definition: Relating to or denoting an imagined state or society where there is great suffering or injustice.

Complex story arcs, fear, impending doom and disbelief. Conspiracies abound. Either a world going into dystopia, or an already dystopian world with a bleak backdrop. Everything changes and survival is key; usually fighting against oppressive authority.

(Oryx and Crake by Margaret Atwood, A Scanner Darkly by Philip K. Dick, The Hunger Games by Suzanne Collins, The Handmaid's Tale by Margaret Atwood, Animal Farm by George Orwell)

Paranormal / Ghost stories

Often starts with everyday life, builds up slowly with little things that seem incidental until the characters begin to realise they are intentional – then building on that to create fear and tension, usually before slowly revealing the ghostly or paranormal cause. Set in a spooky abandoned building, a historical house or ancient site. Paranormal romance is a sub-genre of ghost stories which has become incredibly popular.

(Ghost Story by Peter Straub, The Woman in Black by Susan Hill, The Turn of the Screw by Henry James, The Amityville Horror by Jay Anson, Dark Matter, By Michelle Paver, The Woman in White by Wilkie Collins)

Thriller

Begins with action and escalates to become something that must be escaped – a roller coaster of action, fear and tension culminating in an often violent resolution. The purpose of a thriller is to induce the strongest emotional responses possible.

(The 'Jack Reacher' series by Lee Child, Gone Girl by Gillian Flynn, The Widow by Fiona Barton, The Girl on the Train by Paula Hawkins, The Hunt for Red October of by Tom Clancy, A Time to Kill by John Grisham)

Mystery

The scene is set and the mystery is introduced, ensued by a hunt for clues, with everything coming together and the odd 'red herring' (*a fact, idea, or subject that takes people's attention away from the central point being considered*) thrown in to misdirect. A final build-up to the big reveal.

(The Girl with the Dragon Tattoo by Stieg Larsson, And Then There Were None by Agatha Christie, The Hound of the Baskervilles by Arthur Conan Doyle, The Firm, John Grisham)

Historical Fiction

Often detailed descriptions, dialogue is spattered with older language. Full of rich story-telling and 'time-anchors' to enable the reader to really understand the timings. Characters can be historical or fictional. Requires dedicated research by the author to ensure all details are correct for the set period.

(The Other Boleyn Girl by Philippa Gregory, Wolf Hall by Hilary Mantel, The Painted Girls by Cathy Marie Buchanan, Caravans by James A. Michener, The Night Watch by Sarah Waters)

Notes & ideas... ✏️

Week 8

Week 9

Hooks

A narrative hook is a writing technique in the opening of a story that literally 'hooks' the reader in so they feel compelled to continue reading. The length of the 'opening' can be anything from the first few paragraphs of a short story, to the first few pages of a novel, but ideally, it occurs in the opening sentence and 'grabs' the reader immediately.

You need your reader to ask; 'who', 'what' or 'why' as quickly as possible and then keep reading in order to answer that question. **Remember**, your reader has a lot of distractions (social media is your biggest rival).

You could begin your story at a pivotal moment, have an unusual situation, serious conflict or dread.

Hook Exercise 1

- Take a look at a variety of books and see if you can find the intentional hook and rate how effective it is for YOU. Perhaps visit the library and choose a selection of different genre books to see how quickly the hook is set, or are there novels without a discernible hook? Do any particularly 'grab' you?

    Remember, a hook isn't a hook for everyone – for some of your audience it may be the very thing that turns them off your story – you cannot please everyone!

Who is your audience?

The style of your hook will depend on the type of person likely to be interested in your genre of writing. For example, a big explosion probably won't entice someone who enjoys paranormal romance, or chick lit to keep on reading.

What is the purpose of your opening?

- Are you giving the reader a key piece of information (or a clue)?
- Are you presenting a reason for what comes next?
- Are you jumping straight into a piece of action that will get the reader's heart racing and compel them to keep reading?
- Perhaps you are pulling the reader into a world that will fascinate or intrigue them.
- Or maybe you will use unusual terminology (medical or scientific, or 'otherworldly') that will pique the reader's interest.

Whatever the hook, you need to understand your reason for using that particular piece of narrative in order to use it effectively.

Hook Exercise 2

- Create the opening paragraph for a short story in at least three of the following genres. Remember to use different techniques and language, appropriate to the genre. Now test your hook paragraphs on someone else and ask them which ones would make them want to read the whole story.

Romance
Thriller
Fantasy Adventure
Comedy
Science-Fiction
Teen-Angst story

Fairy story
Story for a younger child
Gothic
Ghost Story
A Western

Cliffhangers

A 'cliffhanger' is an unfinished, dramatic or suspenseful situation that leaves the reader on a 'knife's-edge' wondering what will happen next.

The purpose of a cliffhanger is to compel your reader to turn to the next chapter, or to want to come back to your story if they have had to put it down. They are employed at the end of each chapter and, if your book has a sequel, can be used at the end of the book.

(*Note: I keep rattling on about compelling your reader to keep reading – it REALLY IS of vital importance!*)

Some key points about cliffhangers:

- Often the protagonist is left in a precarious situation
- A cliffhanger is often abrupt – a sharp shock
- A cliffhanger need not be a life or death situation, but it should be something your reader will care about
- A cliffhanger can be a setback – a path that is halted and changed by an event.

End of chapter cliffhangers

A cliffhanger doesn't have to be dramatic - although often they are. It can be as simple as an unresolved problem, or an unanswered question that the reader will look forward to finding out what happened.

Will she kiss him? What will be in the package? Did she pass her exam?

A reader will expect a swift resolution, or answer to the cliffhanger in the next chapter. Don't drag it out unnecessarily (or repeatedly) – remember, your reader needs to 'earn rewards' from reading your story by gaining satisfying resolutions as well as unexpected twists.

You need to nurture your reader throughout your story; give and take, let them be right and sometimes prove them wrong with their plot guesses. Play with their emotions, but ultimately leave them satisfied and eager for more.

An open ending

Be cautious about ending a story on a cliffhanger because this can upset the readers who like their tales to be neatly tied up at the end. Some stories end on a 'semi' cliffhanger, in that the reader is left to ASSUME the ending, based on the evidence given. It is a literary technique that can work well in Paranormal style stories, where an air of mystery is expected and in Romance stories where the ending is often left with the characters looking very much like they are going to get together and the author encouraging that assumption, whilst still leaving the details of the ending open to interpretation.

Cliffhanger Exercise 1

- Think of a book you have recently read that you struggled to put down, and then when you did, you couldn't wait to pick it up again. Take a look at the endings of each chapter – what were the cliffhangers that kept you glued to the book?

Cliffhanger Exercise 2

- Cliffhangers can come in many varieties – try writing the last paragraph of a chapter for each one of the list below. You can create new characters and scenarios each time, or use the same characters in different scenarios.

For example: [using Emotional] *He stared at her, tears burning the corners of his eyes. Could he just spit out the words that would change everything for her?*

Emotional	Magical event
Dire peril	Tense situation
Drama	Unexpected arrival
Personal discovery	Sudden disappearance

Week 9

Notes & ideas...

Week 9

Week 10

Frame stories

Framing is a literary method of embedding one story into another – a story within a story. It has the effect of adding layers of complexity to your story; of making it more intricate and therefore (provided you do it skilfully), more interesting to the reader.

How do you add a framework your story?

A simple form of framing is a literary form of placing **'bookends'** at either end of a story. In the opening scene, the narrator introduces readers to important characters and the setting and in the closing scene, brings the story full-circle to the opening scene.

This works well with stories set across multiple generations, where a character from the present can open and close the embedded story (or stories) of their ancestors' past.

This type of framing can also be used to good effect in a story where the survival of the main protagonist is in jeopardy throughout but, the author allows the reader to know they survived (possibly unscathed/possibly not) by virtue of the fact they are recounting what happened. In this case, the story will have started at its endpoint and the narrative takes you back through the events that led up to that point.

A good visual example of this is the movie Titanic, the elderly Rose recounts her tale as a passenger on the tragic ship, crossing the Atlantic Ocean. The reader is then time-slipped into the year 1912 where Rose is a young girl. The elderly Rose interjects to recount her experiences to the reader and the film ends back with the elderly Rose of today, so that even as the story is begins, you know Rose survives.

The film 'The Princess Bride', is story that opens with a grandfather reading a bedtime story to his grandson in the modern day world – the bedtime story is the embedded, main storyline and is set in an enchanted land. Narrative periodically jumps back to interactions between the grandfather and son and film is rounded off with the grandson having enjoyed the story and the grandfather hinting at a possible connection between himself and the fantasy characters in the story.

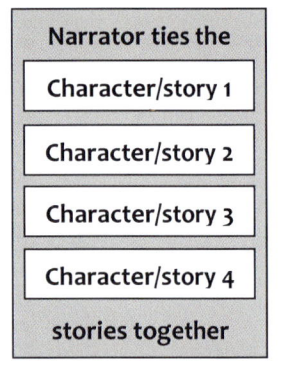

Narrator ties the
Character/story 1
Character/story 2
Character/story 3
Character/story 4
stories together

Multiple narratives: In Canterbury Tales, Geoffrey Chaucer introduces a collection of different characters, each with their own story and distinct character. The pilgrim who meets these characters, links together the various storytellers' narratives and their relationships with each other.

In this type of framework, multiple narratives occur one after another but, in a far more complex frame system, stories can be **'nested'**, whereby the reader is introduced to an embedded story by the narrator and then, a character within that embedded story can take the reader into a further story, or set of stories, before coming back to their own stories.

Narrator opens
Embedded story
Nested story 1
Nested story 2
Double-nested story
Narrator closes

There are no limits to how many times or how complex the framework and nesting can be.

Epistolary tale: this is a story written as a series of documents, such as journals, exchange of letters and even newspaper articles.

Dracula by Bram Stoker is a well-known example and The Jolly Postman by Janet and Allan Ahlberg, where the different stories are told through a series of letters (actual letters in envelopes within the book), delivered by a jolly postman. Other examples are

Bridget Jones Diary by Helen Fielding and The Secret Diary of Adrian Mole by Sue Townsend.

Bookend Frame Exercise

❶ Write a 500 word 'bookend' style frame story. Here are some ideas that you could use, or try one of your own.

Do feel free to change the character names.

❶ Talli is about to get married, but an event from her past has to be reconciled before she can walk down the aisle. Use the 'bookends' to show her before the wedding and after the wedding (if she goes through with it). The embedded story should be that of her childhood event, showing the reader why she is struggling with her decision at this point in her life.

❷ Max was pronounced dead at eleven-hundred hours – one hour after he said 'I do' to Louise. The ghost of Max is narrating the days or hours up to his death and the answer to 'who killed him?'

❸ Adoptee, Elspeth has been sent a box of letters from an unknown source. The letters tell the story of her, as yet unknown, past.

Epistolary Tale Exercise

❶ From your local newspaper, find a 'reader's letter' that feels like there could be an ongoing saga and create a 500 word story through a series of linked letters that appear in a paper.

Or, check the 'searching for love' advertisements and create a story around the posts and the people posting them.

If you fancy doing something a bit different, get an A4 sheet of paper and paste several cut-out letters from newspapers onto it and create a visual story, adding your own writing to link the stories or items. There is an example on the next page.

Get your Fortune Told With mystic Cristi

👁

Your appointment is at: 3.15pm

Journal entry: Monday 5th May

Went to visit a psychic today – it was weird, she told me I could not marry my fiancé and that I had to find out the truth about my past. Am about to phone mum to ask her

---

Journal entry: Wednesday 7th May

So…it's taken me a couple of days to get my head together enough to actually put this into words. I still can't believe it. I was adopted. My real last name is not Sutteridge. Mum (she'll always be mum to me) said she was dreading this day.
What the HELL!! She says my name was changed but the adoption people wouldn't tell her what from – I came to them as a new-born.

Journal entry: Monday 12th May

Harris has been great, he said he'll help me find out who my parents really are. He truly is my soul-mate, no matter what that silly psychic says.

> I found my birth certificate...

Does it say who your parents are?
Are you ok - text me as soon as you know
I love you xxx

> We need to talk - now, can you come over?

I'll come right away - do you need wine?

CERTIFICATE OF BIRTH

Name and Surname: Angela Brown
Sex: female
Date of Birth: 25th September 1976
Place of Registration: Crowborough

Journal entry: Thursday 15th May

I can't believe it – Harris and I have the same last name. A worrying thought comes to me and I am hoping that I can prove myself wrong.

Journal entry: Tuesday 23rd June

I haven't been to work for a week. Harris has stopped calling and mum keeps leaving frantic messages. I should not have looked into my past…Funny…no, NOT really funny because I guess I Harris and I have a stronger bond than most couples, which I put down to luck – not biology.
He never knew his dad and his mum never talks about him.

LOCAL SAM
BROWN GUI
OF MURDER
2 DAUGHTE

Sat 27th June

I finally sent a message to Harris. It was smudged with tears, but he has to know the truth. His father killed my mother and sisters. She was his second wife, after Harris' mother. No wonder she won't talk about him.

Week 10

Notes & ideas...

Week 10

Week 11

Colour a scene

When you describe a setting, the way you describe it depends on your own personal perspective. People often see places very differently from each other, for example; the forest glade below may appear appealing and friendly to one person, but to someone else, who may have had a bad experience in the woods, or just feel more comfortable with urban settings, it could look like a scary or spooky place to be.

Photo by Lucie Hošová on Unsplash

I have taken the same photograph and applied three different filters to it. How does each one make you feel about the scene?

Who could you imagine there and what would they be doing?

As an example, in the original photo, I would imagine a woman walking her dog.

The warm-colour photo (top-right) reminds me of Centre Parcs and I could see a family with two young children and a small dog frolicking.

Bottom-left makes me think an alien spaceship could be hovering above.

Bottom-right is slightly sepia and I could see a couple of ghostly Edwardian children walking down the path.

When you describe a setting, remember to describe the colours – like the filters I have used above, this will affect its atmosphere and how it 'feels' to the reader – remember, the reader cannot see the image in your head unless you describe it to them.

What sounds might you hear? Is it silent or noisy – be specific with background noises that will add to the overall sense of the place. **What would you feel?** Is it cold, is there a breeze blowing round your ears, are there biting bugs, prickly branches, feathery ferns tickling your legs? **What can you see?** Gentle bumble bees or nasty gnats, friendly foxes or snarling vermin, playing dogs, lovely songbirds or 'Hitchcock's birds'?

Scene colour Exercise 1

📌 Write a couple of paragraphs to describe each of the forest scene photographs, using colour, shade and tone to set the atmosphere.

You could put yourself or another character/s into some of the scenes and describe the scene from their point of view.

Scene colour Exercise 2

📌 Visit some different locations, both indoors and out with a notepad to hand and write down a factual account of what you see, what you can hear, what you can feel and what you can smell.

Next, decide on a specific 'mood' for the setting – is it going to be happy, spooky, romantic, mysterious or dangerous? Now re-write the description of the location, 'colouring' all aspects of it to take on the mood you have designated to it.

For example: *The museum was an opulent building, with wooden panels and velvet adorning every surface. Glass cabinets displayed Victorian clothes and the musty scent of damp permeated the air.*

With a spooky mood: *The opulence of the past shrieked entitlement through the echoing wooden panels that hid secret doorways and fingerprints of those long dead. Velvet seats, now threadbare, still bore indentations, as if someone invisible was sitting next to me, while I half expected the musty-clothed mannequins to re-animate under the shadowy Victorian lamps.*

Or, with an excited mood: *The building was vast, crammed with precious treasures each screaming for my undivided attention. Indentations on the velvet viewing benches told of a many a visitor, equally enthralled with the gorgeous gowns and adornments of our past.*

Notes & ideas...

Week 11

Week 12

Thinking about writing for children

There are some key points to bear in mind when writing for children. One of them is that fiction for children is defined by age-specific categories, because what interests an eight-year-old could seem childish and boring to a twelve-year-old. There are various definitions, depending on whether you look at the American or English markets – below are examples of the age-group categories (I have combined several different lists to give a broad example:

Board books: New-born to age 3

Picture books: Ages 0-5 or 3-8

Early readers: Ages 5-7 or 5-9, these are for children who are just beginning to reading independently. They are short and usually illustrated.

First chapter books: Ages 6-9 or 7-10, the stories are divided into about ten equal sized chapters and have with a word counts of no more than about 10,000 words. The *Rainbow Fairies* series is a good example.

Middle-grade books: Ages 9-12, Chapter stories with between 30,000 and 60,000, though often more towards the smaller figure.

Young teen: Age 12-15 Word counts of up to around 70,000 words (a bit longer if its science fiction).

Young adult (YA) novels: Ages 14 and up YA books usually feature a teenage protagonist, despite the fact that many of the readers are actually adults. A similar expected word count to Young teen.

Younger children generally prefer stories with safe, happy endings, whereas older children can cope with more uncertainty or danger on the way to the ending

Before you write a story for children, think about the stories you loved at the age you want to write for and look at what is available for that age now. Google the age category and read some of those books to get a good understanding of current themes and which stories have endured the course of time and why?

It is particularly important to understand the children's book market because, at this age, it is not just the children whose tastes you are catering too, but also the parents and grandparents who are buying the books for them and often reading them to them too. And remember:

- Don't talk (or write) down to children.
- Keep plots simple, but don't 'dumb them down', just make sure you explain things more fully for the younger child.
- Use complex words, but in a context where the child can work out the meaning.
- Know that children and adults often find different things funny.
- Don't over-complicate scene set-ups.
- Characters need to jump off the page and grab the child's attention fairly swiftly, so there isn't time for long really long backstories.

Writing for children Exercise 1

Read **Madeline** by Ludwig Bemelmans (first published in 1939) and, or **The Gruffalo** by Julia Donaldson (first published in 1999) – two of the most loved rhyming books of recent and past times. They differ from each other in both topic and style, so what is it that makes them so popular?

As a parent, I can tell you that they are both pleasing to read aloud and easy to memorise. Personally, I feel that rhyming books have a soothing effect on both the parent and child.

Write a story in rhyme for the 0-5 age group. Make sure the rhymes are smooth and the lines flow. Read it aloud and wherever you stumble over the words, make adjustments to smooth it out. A parent will not enjoy reading awkward rhymes – and you have to please the parent as much as the child!

Writing for children Exercise 2

📌 Thinking about First Chapter books – this is an area with a lot of possibilities because at this stage, children love consistency and 'more of the same'. Which means that there is a great opportunity to write a chapter book series, rather than just one book.

Take a look at the **Rainbow Magic** books (of which there are over two hundred). These books are incredibly popular with the 7-9 age group and feature the same main characters and a formulaic plots involving goblins doing bad things and various fairies fixing the problem. The same applies to the Animal Arc series, Judy Moody and many of the Enid Blyton Famous Five and Secret Seven books.

Take a look at some of these books and other First Chapter books that you find in the library or on Amazon and make a list of characters and situations they cover:

Book Series	Characters	Theme
Rainbow Magic	Two girls who turn into fairies, fairies and goblins.	Fairies saving the day from disaster brought on by the goblins.
Animal Arc	A young girl, whose parents are vets and her best friend, various different animals.	Finding animals in trouble and trying to help them.
Judy Moody	A young girl, her brother Stink and friends.	A strong and adventurous character getting into mishaps and having adventures.
Beast Quest	A boy and a girl, magical beasts.	Fighting beasts on magical adventures.

Now try plotting your own idea for a children's series using the 'five finger pitch' from the beginning of this course.

Week 12

Notes & ideas...

Week 12

One last thing

Rich Writing Bingo Card

Whenever you write a story, it is worth checking it has enough 'ingredients' to bring it to life for your reader.

If you can, get someone else to read your story out loud, or read it yourself into the voice recorder on your phone and play it back to see what you have, what is clear, what is unclear and what you might be missing.

Are each of these things clear in your story?

Main Character (protagonist/PoV)	The Goal (aim or desire)	The Obstacles (conflict)	Solution (resolution)	Clear Theme and/or Setting

What is the perspective of your story?

Past Tense has already happened	Present Tense happening now	1st Person POV I, we me, my, our pronouns	3rd Person POV She, he, they, them pronouns	2nd Person POV You, your, yours

Does your story contain (*at least 4 of these*)?

Sounds	Humour	Emotions	Colourful descriptions	Smells
Conflicting characters	Physical sensations	Tension	Dialogue	Unexpected twists

Plots & Masterplans

Novel ideas

Stories I must write

Writing competitions

Date Entered	Competition details	Results Announced

Writing competitions

Date Entered	Competition details	Results Announced

Printed in Great Britain
by Amazon